The (NEARLY)
Teenage
GIRL'S
GUIDE
to (ALMOST)
Everything

Author: Dr Sharie Coombes
Illustrator: Lindsey Sagar
Additional text by: Marnie Willow and Claire Sipi
Editor: Helen Catt
Designer: Richard Sykes
Index: Elizabeth Wise

An imprint of Igloo Books Group,
part of Bonnier Books UK
bonnierbooks.co.uk

Published in 2019
by Igloo Books Ltd, Cottage Farm
Sywell, NN6 0BJ

Manufactured in China. 1019 001
10 9 8 7 6 5 4 3 2 1

Library of Congress Cataloging-in-Publication
Data is available upon request.

ISBN 978-1-83852-387-9
autumnpublishing.co.uk
bonnierbooks.co.uk

The (NEARLY) Teenage GIRL'S GUIDE to (ALMOST) EVERYTHING

AUTUMN PUBLISHING

CONTENTS

iNtRODUCtiON

What is puberty, when will it happen and why is it happening to me?

Puberty is a period of time when your body and mind are preparing for adulthood. It's the start of a phase of your life called adolescence, when you grow more quickly than you have since the year you were born.

Puberty doesn't happen overnight or at the same time for everyone, but it does **happen to everyone**. Your favorite sports people, writers, and musicians have all been through it. Even your parents and teachers went through it. Your body will probably still be changing until your early twenties.

There might be days when it's hard. You might feel really grown up but at the same time, still very attached to things you loved when you were younger. **Don't worry**, it's the same for everyone. **You're not alone,** so ask if you need support and encourage your friends to do the same.

Your friends will be going through this too.

They may need your support at times.

When will it happen?

Puberty happens in its **own time,** as we're all different. For some people, it starts in the last few years of elementary school. For others it may begin in the last few years of middle school, or **anywhere in between.**

Girls often start puberty a year or so earlier than boys. On average, girls are about 11 when things start changing, while boys are around 12. Puberty might seem like it lasts for ages, but this is a good thing, as it gives you **time** to get used to the changes in your body, your new likes and dislikes, feelings, behavior, and ways of thinking. **Remember**, you'll still be **you** after puberty, but with more skills, experience, and strength.

What will happen to me, and why?

You'll experience changes in all parts of your life:

Body   CHANGES   Brain

Behavior   Mind

Body: Chemicals called **hormones** are made by your brain and body. Your body responds to new hormones created during adolescence by **gradually becoming an adult body.**

Brain: Your brain will be working hard to make space for new pathways, so you can learn challenging new things. Your memory will get a boost, too. You'll probably need **a lot more sleep** while your brain is making these changes.

Mind: You'll develop new likes and dislikes, needs, and interests. You might notice you experience more moods, and your feelings may become **stronger** and **more intense.**

Behavior: Friends and fitting in can suddenly feel much more important than they used to. It's important to **stay connected** to your family, who are there to support you as well.

List the things that interest or worry you about puberty:

Share your list with someone you trust if you are worried about anything. Don't worry in silence.

HORMONES

Your body is controlled by chemical messages that travel around in your blood. These chemicals are called hormones and, among other things, they give the signal for your body to start going through puberty.

Chemical control

Hormones don't just control things to do with puberty. Your body produces about **fifty** different hormones that tell it how to grow, when to eat and how to process food, when to sleep, and loads of other things. They control your body's response to **danger**, too.

If you find yourself shaking with fear or anger, that's thanks to a hormone called **epinephrine**, which prepares your body to fight or run away from threats.

Blame game

Hormones get a bad rap. They often get **blamed** for everything that happens during puberty, including bad moods, intense emotions, and impulsive behavior. But scientists now know that most of these things are caused by changes in your **brain** that happen around adolescence. Hormones aren't the enemy. They're just part of your body doing what it needs to do.

HORMONES ARE LIKE CHEMICAL MESSAGES

ow it works

Hormones are made in little organs called **glands** that are found around your body and brain. When your body is ready to start puberty, a gland called your **pituitary** releases the hormones that kick the process off. This tiny, pea-shaped organ is located at the bottom of your brain, in an area called the **hypothalamus**.

The start of puberty is a bit like a line of **dominoes** falling over. First, the hypothalamus starts producing a hormone called **gonadotropin releasing hormone** (GnRH). This builds up in your bloodstream.

When the level of GnRH is high enough, it signals the pituitary gland to release **two other hormones** called follicle stimulating hormone (FSH) and luteinizing hormone (LH). FSH and LH travel through the blood to your **ovaries** (see page 36), to tell them to start making the hormones estrogen and progesterone. Together, FSH, LH, estrogen and progesterone trigger the physical changes your body goes through during puberty. They also control your **periods**. The levels of these hormones will continue to rise and fall in cycles for as long as you still have periods. For most women, this is until they go through the **menopause** in their fifties.

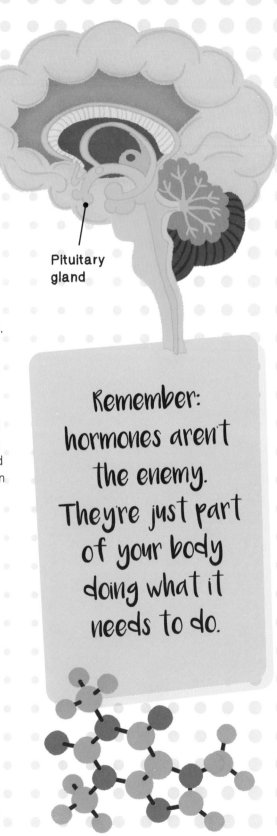

Pituitary gland

Remember: hormones aren't the enemy. They're just part of your body doing what it needs to do.

Physical feelings

Hormones are powerful chemicals. While they're not responsible for everything you feel during adolescence, they can impact your mood in unexpected ways. If you feel edgy or upset or anxious and you don't know why, take a break and do something calming to give yourself a chance to relax. See page 68 for more tips on relaxation.

FEELINGS

What are emotions about?

Your brain is responsible for every thought and feeling you have. Bad feelings sometimes happen whether you want them to or not. The good news is, you can learn to manage them.

When you feel bad, part of your brain is making things harder for you, but only because it wants to keep you safe. **Understand it and help it not to overreact.** Your brain and body **work together.** Give them a high five whenever you can.

Why am I feeling like this?

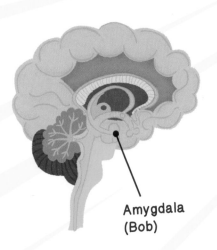

Like everyone, you were born already programmed to feel emotions, like a computer with software preloaded. During puberty, you may have **stronger,** more **intense** emotions and feelings than you're used to.

Emotions happen in the brain in response to a thought, an event, or something you might not even notice right away. They cause a burst of chemicals to pump through your body in seconds.

Feelings are the sensations you notice in your body because of these emotions. **Happiness, courage, satisfaction, sadness, anger,** and **worry** are some feelings you may recognize.

What's Bob got to do with it?

An ancient part of your brain known as the amygdala lives in your limbic system. Let's call it 'Bob'. Bob's job is to keep you safe, and it takes its job very seriously!

Bob handles emotional learning. It behaves like a **guard dog**, pacing around, looking for trouble, and **overreacting** to things it decides are a threat to you, even when they're not. Scientists say that, during puberty, Bob is **busier** and much more **sensitive** than usual.

Amygdala (Bob)

Bob controls your **freeze, fight, flight** response, and can create unpleasant sensations in your body like fear, anger, frustration, and other tricky feelings. It does this by telling your brain there's a danger, which causes stress hormones to be made and pumped through your body. We all get these; it's normal! When you recognize that these feelings are just Bob kicking off, you can learn to manage Bob and make sensible, well-thought-out decisions instead of just reacting.

What Bob might make you feel:

FIGHT
like you want to fight off difficult feelings and people with aggression.

FLIGHT
like you want to run and hide, and avoid tricky issues and situations.

FREEZE
like you're helpless and unable to do anything to escape.

What do I need to do?

You might get fluttery feelings in your chest and stomach when you are excited, happy, worried, or stressed. This is because your heart and stomach have cells that communicate with your main brain all the time. **Look after your body and brain,** because they are **both** important to your happiness and well-being.

Keep your body and brain happy with a high five!

1. **Feed** them right.
2. **Water** them well.
3. **Exercise** them.
4. Give them enough **sleep.**
5. Every day, try to **do something you enjoy** with people who care about you.

What things will you do each day this week that you enjoy?

BRAIN DEVELOPMENT

uring adolescence, your brain works and reacts to the world differently from when you were younger. Neuroscientists say that adolescence is a stage of brain development in its own right.

Your brain will continue to **change** and **develop** through your teen years. Old pathways in your brain get rerouted or redeveloped. This makes room for your brain to make new pathways as you learn from new experiences in your life. You're being **rewired**! This is hard work for you and your brain, so it's hardly surprising if you feel tired, or if you find yourself thinking or feeling different things than when you were younger.

What does my brain do, anyway?

Your brain sends millions of messages every day, even when you're asleep. It's working all the time to make you **smarter** and **better at learning**. Because of your awesome brain, you can speak, plan, learn, adapt, remember, work stuff out, solve problems, find things funny, and understand tricky ideas.

Your brain needs downtime when you are resting and relaxing and doing **nothing in particular**, like daydreaming, doodling, walking or exercising in nature, listening to music, looking at art, or reading your favorite comics, magazines, and books.

Give your brain an easier time by eating well and staying hydrated. Drink a few glasses of water throughout the day so the messages have an easier journey.

Why do I sometimes feel up and down?

During adolescence, your brain systems will be **temporarily** out of sync with each other while they reorganize themselves and the way they manage your emotions. Your limbic system (see page 9) might overreact, so you may feel happy one minute and really sad, worried, or angry the next. This will pass. **It's just Bob** barking at you.

In addition, the **hormones** responsible for the physical changes in your body can confuse your developing brain. It hasn't gotten used to having so much of them swooshing around. Bob is particularly sensitive to these hormones.

On top of that, your brain also makes chemicals to control your moods. Mood swings happen because your brain doesn't know how much of these chemicals to make now that you've got more hormones floating around. It learns quickly, but you can help it out by practicing calm breathing and relaxation skills (see page 68 for some ideas).

There may be times when you feel confused, upset, or worried by some of the changes you notice. **Don't worry**, this won't last and you will feel 'normal' again soon. If it feels like it's taking too long for you to feel ok again, talk to an adult and make an appointment to see a doctor so you can get some help to feel better.

Memories are made of this

The experiences you have now will help to **shape your brain,** and you will still remember them well into your adulthood. Your brain is especially good at remembering emotional moments in adolescence and adapting to help you learn from them. You might hear people say your brain is 'plastic' at this age. That means it changes to suit the environment around you so you can fit in and be safe.

Doing things you enjoy with your family and friends will help your brain to develop healthily. So go ahead and **do something fun!** Maybe grab some popcorn and watch a movie or play a game.

List the ways your brain is unique to you. What fascinates or angers you?

Like your fingerprints, your brain is unique and individual. Some of us have a brain that is wired slightly differently than most, which can result in things like autism (ASD), dyslexia, Tourette's Syndrome, or ADHD. This can make people more creative, impulsive, anxious, or self-sufficient. We call this neurodiversity.

WHY AM i SO ANGRY?

Feeling angry sometimes is a normal, healthy response to some situations. It may be that something is (or seems) unfair, confusing, or embarrassing. It may be you're unable to manage your feelings in that moment. Or it may be because you believe you are powerless, not taken seriously, or feel trapped in a situation you don't like. Anger can build up over time and take you by surprise.

We all have to learn to control our anger as we get older so we don't damage important relationships or frighten other people. Uncontrolled anger is harmful to you and to people around you. It's ok to feel angry and you can do that without acting out.

Shouting, destroying or breaking things, lashing out, or physically hurting or insulting others are ways people sometimes act out. Others may turn their anger in on themselves and take it out on their body, their thoughts, or their self-esteem. All of these might be a sign that you need to talk to someone and get some support.

When anger overwhelms you, you often can't think straight or see someone else's point of view. You can get into a habit of giving in to angry thoughts or behavior, which will make you feel worse. Getting anger under control can feel very difficult, but it's possible with support, and it will make you feel happier.

What's happening to me?

Your body and brain go through some big changes in just a few seconds when you get angry. Your heart will beat harder and faster in your chest, your stomach might twinge, you might clench your mouth and fists, your whole body might feel tense and out of control. It's important to try to notice and recognize these warning signs so you can take control.

Your thinking brain (pre-frontal lobes) goes into hiding and you might behave dangerously or do things you regret because your amygdala (Bob) thinks it's fighting for your life.

We become functionally stupid when we're angry and we can't call on our usual logic and intelligence. We're drowning in brain chemicals that hide our true thoughts so we can survive the moment. This was really important for humans in the Stone Age, but we don't face the same threats now, so we have to train our responses.

Getting control

When you feel your anger stirring, there are things you can do. One of the most important ways to get control is to have a plan together for learning to manage your anger. Talk to someone about how to do this. It could be a parent, school counselor, or therapist.

Tips for keeping your cool:

Know your warning signs.

Walk away. Either find somewhere to sit until you're calm or do something energetic.

Breathe deliberately in for 3 and out for 5. Keep going until Bob stands down.

Think about something pleasant, or count to 10, or 100.

Have a drink of water. This fast-tracks Bob into normal behavior.

Get help if you need it.

GRRR!

If you find that you are getting angry more often, or that the anger starts to feel more difficult to manage, you can see a counselor who will help you to find strategies that work for you. Talk to an adult you trust to arrange this support, or contact one of the help lines or websites in the resources section of this book.

we are family

Scientists have discovered that feeling like we are part of a group or family makes our bodies and minds feel comfortable and content. We all need to feel that we are safe, lovable, and wanted. Family can help you work out who you are and support you through tricky times.

Families come in all shapes and sizes, and there is **no such thing** as a **'normal'** or **perfect family**. Not all children grow up with their own family for lots of different reasons.

You might feel completely different from other members of your family, or as though they don't understand you. Families frequently **fall out** and **make up**, often many times a day. Taking time to **listen, think,** and **be kind** can really help everyone to get along much more easily.

Why do I find them so annoying?

As a teenager, you may find that you have a lot of new and contradictory feelings about all sorts of things, including your family. This is normal and part of growing up.

You may want to practice being **in charge** of your own life but, at the moment, you probably don't have all the skills and experience you need to be fully independent yet. It can feel **really frustrating**. You may also feel more sensitive about issues like privacy as you learn to set your own boundaries.

Not only that, but your brain finds it hard to read situations well when you're upset or angry. You might feel **criticized** when an adult explains or suggests a different way of doing something. Remember, no one has all the answers; that includes you, and also the adults around you. Sharing experiences and ideas and working together is often the fastest way to improve your relationship, for both of you.

You might be furious with your family about something and at the same time, want them to give you a hug. This is **completely normal**. You're getting ready to be an adult, but even adults need and love their family. Be ready to laugh whenever these contradictions happen and you'll all move on quickly.

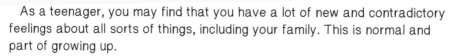

BLOOM WHERE YOU

What are they thinking?

Most parents are **trying** to do their **best** for their children, but it may not always feel that way.

As your body changes and looks more adult, your family might **forget** you're **still maturing** and expect a lot more from you than you're ready for.

As a teenager, you might make more **mistakes** and take more **risks** than you did when you were a child, as you try new things and discover your identity. This can surprise your parents. They might be confused and worried for you as well as upset about what you did. This can lead to arguments and loss of trust, which then needs repairing. Keep **reminding** them you are doing your best. **They are too**.

It can be helpful to get into the habit of telling your family what you're feeling and thinking, so they can better understand **how it feels to be you**. At the same time, you can also try to understand what they are feeling and thinking when they get upset or annoyed. Making sense of your relationships with your parents and your siblings could make you feel much happier, and allow you to support each other through the difficult times.

Putting things right

Don't forget, your family are also trying to get to know the new person you are becoming. You both need to have **patience** and **forgiveness**. Your brain is making things tough for you, but you still have to try to manage your actions and words. Saying **sorry** isn't always easy, but it often makes things better if you can do it.

Spend plenty of time with your family. They will be with you through life's ups and downs. Love and support **go both ways**, so be sure to offer a kind word to your family and look out for when your family members need a hug, too.

Find what works for you as a family. Some people can talk openly about difficult feelings and situations. For others it's harder. If that's true for you and your family, **texting** or **writing** notes to each other might help.

List the places and people who make you feel like you belong...

ARE PLANTED

FRiENDS

In ancient times, it was important to fit in with the rest of the tribe so they would protect, feed, and care for us if we got hurt. Fitting in meant survival. Today, your tribe is the friends you choose to hang out with.

We like to be with people who make us feel good and who share our interests, from music to sports, fashion and a hundred other things. Friends make you **laugh, listen** to your worries, **help** you find solutions, introduce you to **new ideas,** talk about things you **care** about, and make you **feel like you matter**.

Friendships can become **more intense** and feel **more important** during adolescence. If you're lucky, some of the friends you make now might still be your friends in fifty years' time.

When things go wrong and you feel lonely or left out, the hurt feelings you get are as **real** as physical pain from an injury. This can make you lose confidence in your ability to make friends for a while.

IT'S COOL TO BE KIND

What changed?

Adolescence is an **opportunity** to find out who you are and what you like. These things may change several times before everything settles down. Some of your friends may change at the same time and in a similar way. It's an **exciting** time, but it can also be **a bit scary**.

Over time, as your likes and interests change, you might find you have less in common with your old friends. You might want to look for a new group to become part of and for new things to experience. This can be **confusing** for you and for your old friends, who might wonder why you've lost interest in them. Or perhaps your old friends seem to be drifting away and you're left behind feeling lonely, and grieving for the way things used to be.

Falling out

Falling out is **natural**. No two people are identical: we all have likes, dislikes, and experiences that change the way we interact with people. Being exposed to people who think, feel, and act differently to you is a **good** thing. You can **learn** from each other and bounce ideas off each other to come up with **something new**. But disagreements can cause friction, especially when it comes to topics that are **important** to both sides.

Sometimes, one of you may make a **mistake** that leads to a falling-out, doing or **saying** something that the other person finds hurtful. Or you might take offense too quickly at something your friends say or do because you misread what they meant.

Part of growing up is finding ways to **resolve** problems when they arise and being a good friend even while you're arguing.

When you're arguing, try to keep the argument **under control**. Don't let it spiral bigger and bigger. If you find yourself insulting the other person or getting angry, you could try some of the techniques on page 68. Take time to listen to each other's explanations. You each might have a good reason for feeling hurt and angry, and recognizing that can be the first step in making things right. And **be ready to say sorry** if you need to.

Being a good friend

No one is perfect. We are all sometimes selfish, unreliable, or thoughtless. What matters is that you **try** to be a good friend who is **kind** and **considerate**.

If you spot a friend in trouble, offer to help. Just being there to **listen** and **encourage** can be so valuable. **Reach out** to your friend if they seem upset, but recognize that they may want some time alone. Likewise, when you're busy or feeling like you need some time to yourself, tell your friends and let them know you'll be back soon.

If you argue with a friend, don't let resentment build up. An apology or an offer of forgiveness can go a long way. Saying mean things about friends can be tempting but it never helps. If you're upset with a friend, tell them **honestly** and try to work it out. Remember to **be kind** when you do. Encourage your friends to do the same.

Be honest and open about the **good** feelings, too! Tell your friends how much they mean to you and how much you **appreciate** having them in your life. Support their **hopes** and **dreams** and celebrate their **successes**. Have they done something awesome recently? Tell them how great they are!

Not everyone who calls themselves a friend is a friend. Your happiness and self-respect are worth more than a damaging friendship. Find out more on page 21.

ReLatiONShiPS

What is a HEALTHY relationship?

During adolescence, you may develop a romantic or sexual interest in your friends and peers, start dating, and fall in love. When you're dating, the other person becomes your partner, girlfriend, or boyfriend.

A relationship that is beneficial for both of you, makes you feel good about yourself, and is based on respect for yourself and each other is healthy. A healthy relationship allows you to feel comfortable and confident with that person. For that, there needs to be respect between the two of you.

RESPECT MEANS...

... valuing yourselves and each other.

... not trying to have control over the other person or telling them what they can and can't do.

... understanding the other person's boundaries and not putting pressure on them.

What makes a relationship healthy?

Getting along with people we care about isn't always easy, but we have a **responsibility** to treat people well, and a **right** to be treated well too.

Honesty means that you share what you are feeling, thoughtfully and kindly.

Trust helps you to feel safe and sure that the other person won't deliberately embarrass, hurt, or upset you.

Good **communication** means you talk to each other to sort out problems, let each other know how you're feeling, and explain what you need. It includes **compromising** so that one person doesn't always get their own way all the time.

Self-control means that you express difficult feelings in positive ways and don't force your wishes or needs onto the other person.

Kindness is at the heart of every healthy relationship. Giving compliments and doing thoughtful things are great ways to treat people, but there are many ways to be kind.

Walking away

Not all of your friendships and relationships will work out, and there'll be times when relationship isn't right for you. There are lots of ways that you might find that you and our friend or partner are not well-suited. This may well be the case if they often:

- ☒ are not able to consider your feelings
- ☒ upset you
- ☒ do things you don't want them to do
- ☒ ask you to do things you don't want to do

Or it may be that your partner has been respectful and kind, but your feelings for them ave **changed**. Whatever the situation, remember that **you always have the right to walk away.** It's hard to break up, but try to understand that the other person may not vant to stay friends, at least for a while. Explain to them what you're feeling and why, nen give yourself, and them, some space.

> Think about your relationships. Who do you have healthy relationships with? Is there anyone you need to let go of?

Letting go

There may be times when you want to hold on to relationship, but the other person wants to walk way. The loss of a relationship can trigger a **grieving process** as you adjust to the change.

If you're grieving for a friendship or relationship that asn't worked out and you're feeling confused, ask the other person to **explain their feelings**. Even if you an't understand their explanations, try to remember hat it's an experience you can learn from, and that ou will have more relationships in the future.

A big part of what we miss in a relationship is how hat person made us feel, so spend time with your amily and friends who love you, and talk to them as nuch as you need to.

BULLYING

Bullying is the deliberate and repeated use of power by a person or group to hurt or upset others. It doesn't have to be physical power. Bullying can take many forms. Whatever form it takes, it can steal people's peace of mind and happiness.

As long as there have been humans, there's probably been bullying. Something in our survival instinct tempts us to use our **personal power** to feel better about ourselves or protect ourselves by making others feel **less powerful**. Animals also do this, and it's called dominance behavior. Animals fight to be the leader of the pack or in the top dog's group. That doesn't make it ok, though.

We all have the **right** and **responsibility** to speak up about bullying, whether it is happening to us or to others. You won't always be able to manage this without involving trusted adults.

What does bullying look like?

There are four main ways that bullying can manifest:

Verbal:
name-calling, repeated teasing, mocking, **insults,** or **threats.**

Physical or sexual:
pushing or hurting someone, damaging, hiding, or stealing belongings, using their body to **scare** or **hurt** someone, making someone do things that make them **uncomfortable.**

Emotional:
leaving someone out, controlling what they can do, making them look silly, making them **doubt** things they **know** to be true, getting them into trouble, spreading rumors.

Cyber: using technology
to bully, for example by sending unwanted, embarrassing, or upsetting messages; spreading private chats or photos; making threats; or being offensive about someone or their family.

What can I do about bullying?

People who bully others are often looking for a **reaction** to show they have succeeded in exerting their power. If you are being bullied, the best defense is often to be confident, positive, assertive, and resilient. If no reaction comes back, the bully may move on.

Bullies often feel bad about themselves, but act tough to hide it, and **lie** to make you **feel trapped** in the situation.

YOU HAVE MORE POWER THAN YOU REALIZE

Sometimes bullying makes people feel hopeless and like nothing will help, but there is **always** a way to stop it, even if it doesn't feel that way. Talk to important people in your life to get advice or help stop the bullying, whoever it's happening to.

If you experience cyber-bullying, **don't** respond. **Show** the message to someone you trust, even if it's embarrassing. **Block** the bully, **report** them, and **delete** the message.

You can talk to an adult at home, school, or on a help line and make a plan together to end the bullying. Look at the back of this book for resources that may help.

What if I see someone being bullied?

Be an **upstander**, not a bystander, and call out bullying if you see it. Upstanders don't fall for the lies and they go out of their way to support people who've been upset. This can mean getting adult help.

What if I'm the bully?

If you're the bully, you need to **notice, stop,** and **make amends** where possible.

Take **notice** of your behavior, how you interact with people, and how you feel. If you find yourself bullying someone, talk to a friend or adult to help you work out why you have behaved in this way. **Get help** with whatever's been bugging you.

Stop doing it, by walking away if necessary. Find healthier ways to **express** yourself instead.

Make amends: say **sorry**, put right what you can, and maybe even start an anti-bullying campaign to educate others.

WHO AM I?

Adolescence is a time with lots of opportunities to find out about yourself. It's normal to explore your identity and where you fit in. A big part of many people's identity is their gender and sexuality: who they are and who they love.

During adolescence, you'll probably start thinking more about love, sex, relationships, and sexuality. Working out who you are and who you're attracted to can be straightforward and clear from a young age, or it can be confusing and scary. Either way, there might be messy feelings. Sometimes people worry about what others in their family or community will think. Or they may be unsure how to bring up the conversation if they feel different from how others see them or want them to be.

Confusion and anxiety about sexuality or gender are common. It's ok to be **proud** of your differences as well as the ways you are like others. Everyone is **unique**: you'll never be exactly the same as someone else. You get to decide who you are and what matters to you. There's no hurry to 'find yourself' or 'become' you; you're already you from the day you're born, and you will continue to explore, discover, and rediscover things about yourself all your life.

What is sexuality?

Sexuality is who you are sexually and/or romantically attracted to. Lots of people are heterosexual or **'straight'** (men who are attracted to women and women who are attracted to men), but sexuality is **diverse**. Other common identities are covered by the acronym **LGBTQ+.**

Lesbian: a woman who is attracted to and falls in love with other women

Gay: a man who is attracted to and falls in love with other men

Bisexual: someone who is attracted to and falls in love with both men and women

Transgender: someone who identifies as a gender other than the one assigned to them at birth

Queer: an 'umbrella' identity that covers all sorts of ways that people identify, or **questioning,** someone in the process of working out their identity

+ 'plus': a way of including identities such as **intersex** (see page 25), **asexual** (not sexually attracted to other people at all), **pansexual** (attracted to people regardless of their gender), and those who don't want to define their identity.

People often group together under this acronym (or a variation of it) as a way of finding others like them and forging a community. For many LGBTQ+ people, finding their identity is a deeply **liberating and empowering** experience, although it can be difficult at times, too.

If you have any worries about your sexuality or gender, or how others treat you because of them, talk to a trusted adult or contact one of the organizations on the resources page in this book.

What's gender?

When we're born, medical staff record whether we are a girl or boy based on our reproductive organs. Some babies are born with both male and female organs and are recorded as **intersex**.

People who are comfortable with the gender recorded at their birth are known as **cisgender**. Not everyone feels this way. Some people are unsure about their gender for a while. They may spend time with people of another gender and feel more like them than their own birth gender. When those feelings don't change as they get older, it may mean they have gender dysphoria.

If you feel that your **gender identity** is different from what was recorded at your birth, or that you are perceived as a gender that doesn't match your identity, you may be transgender or '**trans**.' Some people are **nonbinary**, which means they don't identify as either male or female, or feel they are both or neither. Sometimes trans and nonbinary people want to change their body to match their gender identity and sometimes they don't. It's an **individual**

choice. Whether or not you're transgender, you may want to dress in clothes you feel match your identity.

Remember, whoever you are and however you identify, you know yourself far better than anyone else in the world does. With or without a label, you're still you, and you are **worthy** of **love**, **friendship**, **respect,** and **happiness**.

Bullying is never ok. Speak to a trusted adult if it happens to you. You don't have to tell them anything about your identity or sexuality. If you're being mean to others because of how you see them, remember how much harm you might do them and stop. Get help to stop if you need it.

LiFe ONLiNe

Technology is a wonderful part of life, where you can share pictures, thoughts, skills, games, music, ideas, and memories with your friends. You can connect with people all over the world who you'd never be able to meet without the Internet.

Being connected doesn't always make us happy. Looking at your friends' lives online, you might think they're having a better or easier time than you. That's probably not true: people often post their 'best bits', like a glitzy shop window full of all the greatest things. Your friends may well be feeling the same way about your life. Comparing yourself with others won't make you happy. You're individual and unique, and so is your life.

Take a break

Growing up these days with access to the world at your fingertips can be great. There's nowhere you can't go, and nothing you can't look up and find out about. Your brain loves to make all these connections and discoveries. It also loves downtime, which gives it a chance to rest and file the information. Remember to spend time away from screens and the Internet, and stick to any screen-time limits set by your family. You might even need to remind your parents to do the same!

Teach your parents something they don't know about social media or the Internet. Adults need skills, too!

If you begin to feel that you can't get through the day without screen time, or if it makes you angry to have to stop, it may be a good idea to talk to an adult and get support to reduce the amount of time you're spending on them.

Think, think, and think again!

Think carefully before you post or send anything. Once it's been sent, you can never take it back. Never let anyone make you do something you don't want to do online.

Content posted online can last forever and could be shared publicly by anyone. Your teacher, parents, or employer could see it, now or at any time in the future.

Surf safe

You have a right to feel safe online and a responsibility to treat others well, just like you do anywhere else. You might feel anonymous behind a screen, but you're not and you are responsible for what you post, say, and do online. You won't always know who you're talking to, so you must be as careful as you would be out in the world. A real friend will never ask you to do anything harmful or dangerous, in real life or online.

Never share your personal information with someone you don't know in person, like your full name, address, or phone number.

Use privacy settings to protect your information.

If you find something online that upsets or frightens you, tell an adult you trust. Don't be embarrassed: it's probably something that they've come across at some point, too.

Use reliable and legal services to access music, film, and TV.

If you get unpleasant messages or you're being bullied, tell an adult. See the section on bullying in this book for more advice.

Delete, block, and report anything that makes you uncomfortable.

If you are shy or have social anxiety, autism, or a disability, online interaction might feel much easier than socializing offline. It's still important to get a good balance of plain old face-to-face human interaction, so make sure you're spending time with family and friends, getting out and about, and doing fun activities.

BODY CHANGES

During puberty, your body goes through a lot of changes. Physically, you are changing from a girl into a woman. By the time you have finished puberty and become an adult, your body will look very different, and will be able to do things that it couldn't before, including having children, if you decide you want them.

your body knows what to do and when to do it.

When does it happen?

Your body will change in gradual stages over about four years, starting about the age of 11. The physical changes don't happen all at once, and for the first couple of years you may not even notice that puberty has begun. You won't suddenly wake up one morning having grown full-sized breasts and sprouted hair in new places! Puberty is like a journey, and it happens naturally at a different pace for everybody, over several years. Your body shape and size is unique to you, and each stage of development will happen when it is right for you.

What changes?

Here is a list of the changes that will happen. All these things will be explained in more detail later on in this book. Remember, the order and time in which these things happen will be different for everyone, so don't worry if some of your friends have already started their periods and you haven't, or if you have to start wearing a bra before some of your classmates. There is no set timetable, and your body knows what it needs to do.

1. Your breasts start to grow. At first, you may notice hard bumps behind your nipples. Over time, these develop and become breasts.

2. You'll start to grow taller, either in one big growth spurt, or in several smaller ones. You'll also get stronger as your muscles develop, and heavier as your body gets bigger.

3. Your hips get wider. This makes it easier and safer to give birth if you ever decide to have children.

4. You grow hair in new places: in your armpits and in the area between the top of your legs. You will also get more hair on your forearms and legs.

5. You start to sweat more, and you'll probably find you need to wash more often. Don't worry, you can wear deodorant to keep the sweat from smelling!

6. Your skin may get oily and cause spots. You'll find some advice for dealing with these on page 34.

7. You start your periods. There is a detailed explanation of this on page 38.

Puberty can be an exciting and a scary time. You might feel self-conscious, proud, worried, strange, and uncomfortable. You might feel all these things at once. This is totally normal, and these feelings will pass. All new things take a while to get used to. By the end of puberty, you will be used to the changes and they won't seem strange any more. Talk to a trusted adult, doctor or nurse if you are worried or have any questions.

HaiR eVeRywHeRe

O ne of the first things you will notice when you start puberty is that you begin to grow hair on your body in places that you didn't have it before. Your new hair develops gradually over several years, and it happens at a different rate for everybody.

You will get pubic hair first, and then about a year later, hair will start to grow in your armpits and on your legs and forearms. It may be the same color as the hair on your head or a different color. Body hair is normal, and everyone has it. And don't worry if your friends get it before you. Yours will grow when your body is ready.

Pubic hair

Pubic hair begins growing in the area between your legs near the top of your labia (see page 36), usually at the same time as your breasts start to grow. There won't be a lot of hair to start with, and it may be light-colored, straight, soft, and fine. As you go through the stages of puberty, it will turn darker, become curlier and coarser in texture, and eventually cover the pubic area (the patch just below your stomach and down to the area between the top of your legs) in a triangular shape.

The good news is that, unlike the hair on your head or face, your new body hair and pubic hair doesn't keep on growing longer and longer. Each hair falls out after about six months, and a new one starts growing in its place.

Other body hair

A little while after your pubic hair starts to grow, you'll notice thicker hair growing in other parts of your body. This will be most noticeable under your arms, in your armpits. But you'll also notice the hair on your legs getting thicker. You might notice the hair on your arms or other parts of your body getting very slightly thicker, too.

Like everything in puberty, hair growth happens at different times and different speeds for everybody. Don't worry if you seem to be developing hair more quickly or slowly than other kids. You can trust your body to get you where you need to be in the end.

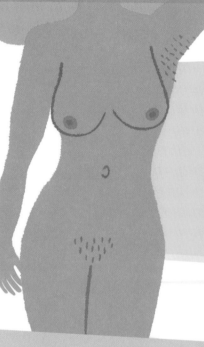

Don't be embarrassed by body hair. Everybody has it!

Hair removal

Body hair can be fair or dark, soft, fine, thick, coarse, straight, or curly. However it looks, it's perfectly natural. Some girls choose to remove the hair from their legs and armpits, or trim their pubic hair. This is an individual choice.

If you are thinking about removing any of your body hair for the first time, talk to an adult, parent, or older sibling for advice on the different ways you can do this. Body hair can be removed by shaving, waxing, or with hair removal creams, or by treatments using lasers or electrolysis to stop hair growth. Any removal process can cause skin irritation, so make sure you choose a method that works for you.

BReaSTS

Breasts come in all shapes and sizes. No shape is wrong, and there is no 'perfect' size. Your breasts won't suddenly appear overnight; they grow slowly during puberty, at different rates for every girl. As they develop, you'll need to wear a bra to keep them comfortable and supported.

What are breasts for?

When a woman has a baby, her breasts start producing milk. This milk is full of everything the baby needs for the first few months of its life: not just food and water, but antibodies that help the baby fight off diseases, and hormones that help the baby grow the right amount. Breasts contain the tissues needed to make breast milk, surrounded by a protective cushion of fat. When the baby feeds, the milk comes out of tiny holes in the nipples.

What to expect

When your breasts first start to grow, you may notice hard bumps behind your nipples. These are called breast buds. They may feel a bit sore or itchy for a while. This is normal, but talk to a trusted adult or a medical professional if you're worried. Once these buds appear, the nipples and the circles of skin around them, called the areola, start to get bigger and a little darker as they develop into your full-sized breasts.

Wearing a bra

You may find it more comfortable to wear a bra to support your growing breasts, especially when you are doing exercise, dancing, or playing sports. A bra stops your breasts moving around uncomfortably and rubbing against your clothes. Not every woman chooses to wear a bra, but most women and girls feel more comfortable if they do.

It's important to get the right size bra. Wearing the wrong size can give you back and shoulder aches and make you very uncomfortable, even if it feels ok when you first try it on. The best way to work out your size is to get fitted at a department store or lingerie shop. These places often provide free fittings, so you don't have to buy anything if you don't ant to. Don't feel shy: the women who work in the fitting rooms really don't care what you look like, and they can usually measure you over your top if you prefer.

There are two parts to a bra's size: band size and cup size. The band size is represented by a number (32, 34, 36 etc.), and measures the part of a bra that runs around your chest and back.

The cups are the parts of the bra that hold your breasts. These are represented by a letter (AA, A, B, C etc.) Your bra size will change a lot of times over your life, not just during puberty.

Rough guide to bra fitting

1. Use a soft tape measure to measure around your rib cage in inches, just beneath your breasts. Round up to the nearest inch. This gives you your band size.

2. Measure around your back and the fullest part of your breasts (this is usually in line with your nipples).

3. Calculate your cup size by taking your band size away from the measurement in step 2. If the two measurements are the same, your cup size is AA. If there is 1 inch difference, it's an A, 2 inches is a B, 3 inches is a C, and so on.

Once you have a rough size, try some bras on to check. You want to check that the band sits straight and doesn't ride up. It should feel comfortable and not too tight: you should be able to fit two fingers underneath it with some resistance.

The part of the bra between the two cups should sit flat against your body without digging into your skin. And the cups should sit smoothly against your body without any wrinkling or sagging. If you get fitted, the fitter can check all these things for you.

There are lots of different styles of bras to choose from. Teen or starter bras are designed to be comfortable when your breasts are first starting to grow. Sports bras provide a lot of support for when you're being active. T-shirt bras are designed not to show beneath your clothes, and you should be able to find one to match your skin tone you want. Underwire bras provide good support for larger breasts, but it's good to avoid them while your breasts are still growing. Pick whatever style feels comfortable.

Spots

There's no getting around it: entering adolescence usually means you get spots. Acne, as doctors call it, is very common during puberty, and can range from slightly annoying to uncomfortable and painful.

Thankfully, acne usually goes away as you get older. And while you will very likely have to put up with it for a few years, there are plenty of treatments available to make spots less uncomfortable and less visible.

What causes spots?

Your skin naturally makes a kind of oil called sebum, which is important for keeping your skin smooth and waterproof. Sebum is produced in sebaceous glands, which sit next to the roots of hairs in your skin, and passes out of your skin through your pores.

However, during puberty, your skin starts to produce a lot more sebum. Some of this extra oil can get mixed with dust, dirt, and dead skin cells. The resulting mess can block the pores, trapping bacteria in the tiny holes, and causing spots to appear on the surface of your skin.

Spots are most likely to occur on your face and neck, and sometimes shoulders and upper body.

1. When pores are clear, sebum oozes out from your sebaceous glands along your hairs to the surface of your skin.

2. If your pore gets blocked, it can appear as a tiny black spot (or blackhead) on the surface of your skin.

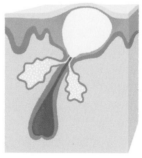

3. If the pore stays blocked, sebum builds up underneath the blockage. This can appear as a white spot (whitehead) on the surface of your skin.

4. If the skin gets irritated or more dirt gets in, the spot can become infected. The area swells up and turns red, and pus develops.

Helping hand

Here are some things you can do to help you take care of your skin and cope with spots:

Never pick or squeeze spots. All you'll do is irritate your skin more, causing more swelling, and risk spreading infection.

Keep your hands and nails clean, and try not to touch or pick your spots.

Keep long hair off your face, as it can irritate the spots.

Wash your face with warm water and a gentle facial wash or cleanser every morning and evening. Avoid soap as this can dry out your skin.

Cover up

your spots are making you feel very ncomfortable and self-conscious, ou can try a medicated concealer o cover them up. Heavy makeup enerally isn't a good idea, though, s it can block the pores even more, nd make your spots worse.

Asking for help

Some people have acne that causes them significant discomfort. If you find your spots painful or are unhappy about them, talk to a doctor or nurse. They may be able to offer medication to get rid of your spots.

GIRLS' BITS

Your reproductive system is the name for the parts of your body that make it possible for you to have a baby. You've always had your reproductive system, but it doesn't become mature and start working until you've started going through puberty.

Most of your reproductive system is hidden inside your body, just above and behind your bladder, and in the area low down on your tummy, inside the protective bones of your pelvis. Knowing what the different parts of your body are called and what they are for makes it easier to understand the changes that are happening.

On the outside

The vulva is the name given to the two sets of 'lips' or labia, the clitoris, and the vaginal opening, located between the tops of your legs.

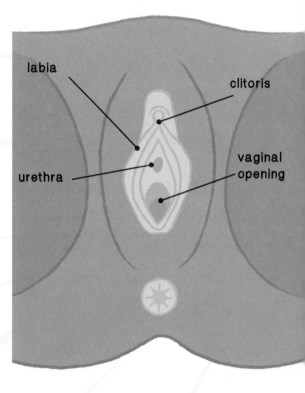

labia

clitoris

urethra

vaginal opening

The outer labia are two thick folds of skin which close over the inner parts of the vulva to protect them. The inner labia are smaller, thinner folds of skin. Between the inner labia are the openings to the urethra and the vagina.

The tip of your **clitoris** is a small bump located at the front of your vulva. This bump is only a small part of the clitoris; the rest of it sits deeper under the skin. It is very **sensitive**, and many girls find stimulating their clitoris results in **sexual arousal** and orgasm.

Your vulva and vagina produce a small amount of fluid to keep them clean and healthy and protect them from infection. You may start to notice it on the inside of your underwear. This is totally normal.

Your vaginal opening may be covered by a thin layer of skin called a hymen. This often wears away while you're still a child, especially if you do a lot of sport. It will wear away completely as you get older.

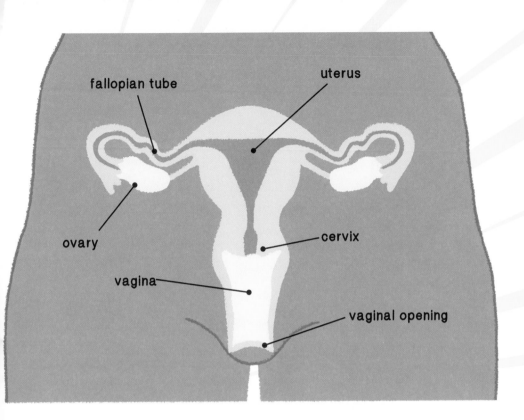

- fallopian tube
- uterus
- ovary
- cervix
- vagina
- vaginal opening

On the inside

You have two **ovaries**, each one about the size of a walnut. Ovaries produce hormones (see page 8) and store **eggs** (or ova). You have all your eggs ready inside your body from the moment you're born, but they do not mature (become ready to make a baby) until you reach puberty. Once you start your **period** (see page 39), an egg is released from one of the ovaries about once a month.

The **ovaries** are joined to the **uterus** by two tubes, called the **fallopian tubes**. When hormones signal the ovaries to release an egg, the end of one of the fallopian tubes catches the egg and pushes it down towards the **uterus**.

The **uterus** (or womb) is where a baby grows when a woman is pregnant (see page 47). It is normally about the size of a small pear, but it stretches to allow a baby to grow to its full size.

The **cervix** is the narrow passageway at the neck of the **womb** that leads to **vagina**. It can stretch open to let a baby pass out of the womb during childbirth.

The **vagina** is a muscular tube that connects the uterus to the vaginal opening between the legs. If sperm enter the vagina, they swim upwards past the cervix to try and join up with an egg in the womb.

Like the **cervix**, the vagina stretches during childbirth to allow a baby to pass through it. Glands inside the vagina produce a fluid that protects the vagina from infection and keeps it clean.

The **urethra** is a tube that carries urine from the bladder, the baglike organ in the body that holds urine, to the outside of a girl's body. It is not connected to the vagina.

PERIODS

At some stage during puberty, you will start having periods. This is the word for the bleeding that happens about once a month from your vagina. It sounds scary, but it's nothing to be worried about.

Most girls have their first period between the ages of 10 and 15. It often happens about two years after your breasts start to develop. Your first few periods might be light (just a few spots of blood) before your period settles into a regular cycle.

What's going on?

Every month, the hormones estrogen and progesterone send a message to your uterus that causes its lining to get thicker. This is so that, if you become pregnant (see page 46), the fertilized egg can attach itself to the lining and develop into a baby. If there is no fertilized egg, the lining breaks away and bleeds a little. The blood seeps slowly out of your vagina, and this is your period. The bleeding usually lasts 3 to 7 days.

It takes around 28 days for the uterus lining to build up and break away. This process is called the menstrual cycle. You count it from the first day of one period to the day before the next one starts. You might want to keep track of your period in a diary or on an app, so you can work out when to expect your next one.

What to do

There are lots of different products you can use to soak up the blood. The easiest to deal with are probably sanitary pads. These are like very thin sponges that you can stick inside your underwear. You'll need to change them every few hours, depending on how heavy the bleeding is. Even if the bleeding is light, it's good to change them often so the blood doesn't start to smell and so bacteria don't build up. You can get pads in different sizes and thicknesses, and you'll probably want a thicker one for overnight.

You could also use tampons, which are thin, absorbent pads that you insert into your vagina. Like sanitary pads, they come in different sizes, depending on the heaviness of the bleeding.

Tampons come with instructions that tell you how to insert them. The first time you use one, read the instructions carefully. They will include a section about toxic shock syndrome. This is a rare but serious bacterial infection that can very occasionally occur if you use tampons. Seek medical help immediately if you get two or more of the following symptoms: high temperature, sore throat, dizziness, headache, muscle pain, an unusual rash, diarrhea, or vomiting.

There are other options, too, such as menstrual cups and specially designed underwear. Try different options and decide what works best for you.

tampon

sanitary pads

What do periods feel like?

Different girls will experience periods differently. Some girls barely notice them, some find them mildly uncomfortable, and some girls feel very unwell. You may feel uncomfortable as your womb tightens up during your period. This feels like aches or cramp in your stomach. You may also find that you experience more severe mood swings in the days leading up to your period.

What can help?

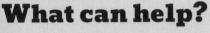 If you're getting mild cramps, doing some gentle exercise may help.

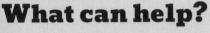 Hot water bottles may help ease cramps.

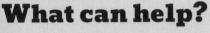 Taking a painkiller, such as ibuprofen, can help. Speak to your parents or a health professional before taking any medication.

 Try to eat a healthy diet. Big sugar spikes and crashes can make you feel worse.

 If you're feeling a bit sad or vulnerable, do something nice for yourself. Have a long hot bath, read a book, cuddle a pet, or try one of the relaxation activities at the back of this book.

If your period feels very uncomfortable, or if you have to keep missing days from school because you feel so unwell, talk to your doctor or another health professional. Don't be embarrassed, and don't suffer in silence.

What about Boys?

Boys experience puberty differently from girls, but it starts in a similar way, with hormones released by their brains that trigger a number of physical changes. Just like girls, these changes can happen quickly or slowly, they can feel like big changes or be barely noticeable.

Puberty for boys can start when they are about 10 or 11. For most boys, it kicks in around the age of 12, and the biggest changes take place between the ages of 13 and 15, although some may take a bit longer.

What changes?

Boys' bodies go through some of the same changes that girls' bodies do, and some that are different. Like girls, their bodies are changing in a way that gives them the ability to have children, should they want them, as well as transforming from a child to an adult. These changes happen at different times; there is no set timetable. Here's what happens to a boy during puberty:

1. His face and body gets hairier. He grows hair in new places, such as in his armpits and around his groin. This usually starts with his pubic hair, just as it does for girls, followed by armpits and facial hair. He'll also get hairier on his chest, arms, and legs. In general, men have more hair than women, but this varies from person to person.

2. He grows taller, either in several smaller growth stages, or as one big growth spurt. Boys also get heavier and stronger. Girls' growth spurts generally start a bit before boys', so you may notice you get a bit taller than the boys in your class. They'll soon catch up.

3. His voice gets deeper, and he'll develop a bulge in his throat called an Adam's apple. This happens when his voice box gets bigger. This can be a gradual process, or quite sudden. His voice may crack or squeak while his body is adjusting. It's not unusual for boys to feel a bit self-conscious about this.

4. His penis and testicles grow bigger, and he'll start to get erections. Erections happen when signals in a boy's brain send a message to make extra blood flow into his penis. This makes it get larger and stick straight out from his body. It's the body's way of preparing them to have sex. During puberty erections can happen a lot, often for no reason.

5. He'll start to produce semen, a whitish fluid that comes out of the end of his penis. This fluid contains millions of sperm cells, too tiny to see. It is these sperm that fertilize an egg in a girl's body when she becomes pregnant.

6. He'll start to sweat more and may need to wash more frequently.

7. His skin may get oily, and he may get spots on his skin.

BOYS' BitS

Going through puberty means your body is getting ready to have children. It's the same for boys, although their bodies change in different ways. During puberty, a boy's penis and testicles get bigger and start to behave in new ways.

On the outside

The penis has two main parts, a **shaft** and a **head** (called the glans). The glans is protected by a fold of skin called the **foreskin**, which can roll back.

The penis doesn't have any bones or muscles in it. Normally it is soft and hangs down. When a boy is sexually excited, the penis becomes hard and points out. This is called an **erection**.

The scrotum hangs outside the body, behind the penis. **Testicles** are egg- shaped balls of tissue that hang inside the scrotum. They are where sperm and hormones are produced.

On the inside

A tube called the **vas deferens** connects the testicles with the urethra. Sperm travel down this tube in a liquid called **semen**, into the urethra, and out of the end of the penis This is called **ejaculation**. If sperm enter a woman's vagina, she can become pregnant (see page 46).

The **bladder** is a baglike organ that stores urine. The **prostate gland** is located just below the bladder, surrounding part of the urethra. It produces a liquid that helps to make semen, and helps to push semen out of the penis when the boy ejaculates.

The **urethra** is the tube that carries urine from the bladder to the end of the penis. Semen also leaves the penis through the urethra, but muscles around the bladder make sure that semen and urine can never come out of the penis at the same time.

Just like girls, boys all look a little different down there.

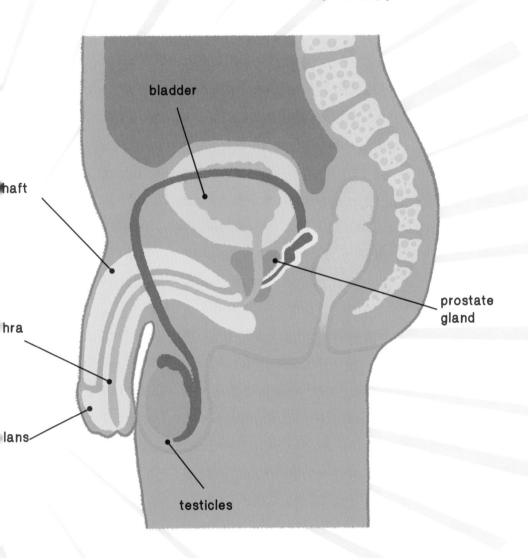

bladder

haft

hra

lans

prostate gland

testicles

Circumcision

All boys are born with a flap of skin called a **foreskin**, which protects the sensitive tip of their penis from bumps and bruises. However, sometimes, usually for **cultural** or **religious** reasons, this skin is **removed** shortly after birth, in an operation called a **circumcision**.

sex

Why am I having sexual feelings and thoughts?

The hormones that are produced during puberty may also make you have sexual feelings and thoughts. You will probably feel more curious about your own body and you may start to feel physically attracted to other people.

Whether you are attracted to girls or boys or both (see page 24), this is the stage of your life when you may want to begin to explore your **sexual feelings**. It will probably be a while before you are ready to **share** these feelings physically with another person, but it's important to understand them.

It is **normal** to feel a bit embarrassed talking about sex, or to worry what your **sexual feelings** might mean. If you have any questions or worries, **talk** to someone you trust. Remember, any adult will know what you are going through, because they've been through it, too!

What is sex?

Having sex with someone usually means giving each other sexual **pleasure**. Your first physical relationships will probably involve **kissing** and **cuddling** with someone you're attracted to. Over time, as you grow older and your relationship becomes deeper and more **trusting**, you may feel ready to move on to more intense sexual activity.

Whatever you decide to do, there are things you must know about to **protect** yourself and your partner. Understand the **law**: sexual activity below a certain age is illegal. Protect yourselves from **infections** and **pregnancy**. And understand your and your partner's **boundaries**. You'll find more information about all these things on the following pages.

Why do people have sex?

People mainly have sex because it **feels good**, especially if it is with someone they really care about.

Kissing, rubbing, and touching someone else makes you and them feel **sexually aroused** (excited) and one or both of you may have an **orgasm**, an intense feeling of pleasure across your body.

People may also have sex because they want to have a **baby** (see page 46). During **sexual intercourse**, a man puts his penis inside a woman's vagina. If they are not using contraception (see page 48), this can make the woman **pregnant**.

Am I ready?

Just because you might be having sexual feelings, it doesn't mean you **have** to have sex or that you are ready to do it. Sex isn't just a physical experience. It often brings **intense emotions** with it. You may be physically ready to have sex before you feel emotionally and mentally ready.

NEVER do anything you **don't want** to, or **pressure** anyone else to do something they don't want to do. Even if some of your friends are having sex, or say they are, **don't feel rushed** into doing it before you're ready. Sex with the right person can be **wonderful**, but with the wrong person or at the wrong time, it can be **unhappy** or even harmful. See page 52 for more information.

> Masturbation is when you touch yourself for sexual pleasure. It is a good way to find out what you like before you have sex with another person. It is safe, feels exciting, and helps you understand your own body's needs.

Trust and respect are essential in any relationship that involves sex.

Pornography

Pornography, or 'porn,' is the word for sexually explicit videos or pictures. Whether or not you're looking for it, it is likely you'll encounter pornography **online** at some point. If so, there are some **important things** to be aware of.

Pornography is designed to **look good** on-screen, **not** to be **safe, comfortable, or fun** for the people involved. It's definitely not a model to try and imitate. **Never** feel that you need to look or behave like a porn star in your own sexual activity, or that you're 'inadequate' if you don't. And **never pressure anybody** else to behave that way during sexual activity.

PREGNANCY

Pregnancy begins when an egg produced by a woman is fertilized by a sperm produced by a man. Over the course of nine months, the fertilized egg divides and develops into an embryo, then a fetus, then eventually a baby that is born into the world.

When a man **ejaculates** during sexual intercourse, semen, containing hundreds of millions of **sperm**, is released into the woman's vagina. The sperm swim towards the **fallopian tubes**.

If one of the **sperm** meets an **egg** from one of the woman's ovaries, it enters the egg and fertilizes it, creating an embryo. If the embryo then implants itself in the lining of the woman's **uterus** (womb), the woman becomes pregnant.

Unless you are using **contraception**, sexual intercourse between a man and a woman **always** carries the possibility of pregnancy. If you are not ready to raise a child, it is important FOR BOTH PARTNERS to use contraception. See page 48 for more information.

A pregnancy is divided into three phases called **trimesters**:

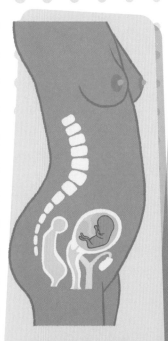

1ST TRIMESTER:
from conception to the end of week 13.

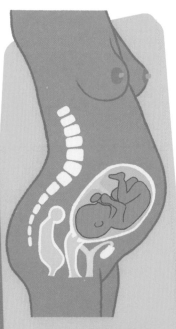

2ND TRIMESTER:
from week 14 to the end of week 26.

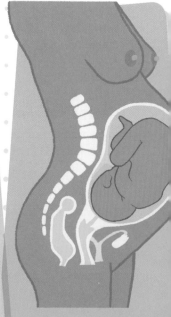

3RD TRIMESTER:
from week 27 to the end of the pregnancy.

How the fetus develops

Once an egg has been **fertilized** by a sperm, it forms an **embryo**. The embryo attaches itself to the wall of the **uterus**. Here it begins to develop into a **fetus**.

As the fetus develops and grows bigger, it is protected by the **uterus** and a liquid called **amniotic fluid**, which surrounds it inside the womb.

An organ called the **placenta** provides all the oxygen and nutrients that the developing fetus needs. The placenta grows into the wall of the uterus and joins to the fetus by a tube called an **umbilical cord**.

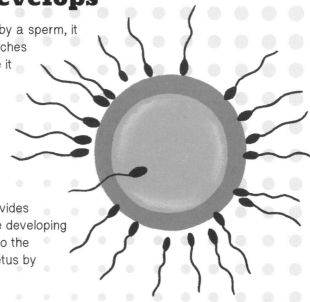

Birth

A pregnancy lasts about **40 weeks**. This is how long it takes for the baby to develop from an embryo to a fetus, and into a baby ready to be **born**.

When the time comes, the muscles in the wall of the woman's uterus start to **contract** (squeeze together) and the **cervix** (the opening of the uterus) starts to open. The **contractions** push the baby out of the uterus and out of the woman's body through the vagina.

Once the baby is born, medical staff will cut the **umbilical cord** so that the baby is no longer attached to it. The **placenta** breaks away from the uterus wall and more contractions push it out of the vagina.

If you have any questions about pregnancy, talk to a doctor or nurse, or your parents, or another adult you trust.

What if a woman doesn't want to be pregnant?

If a woman becomes pregnant **accidentally** or unexpectedly, and doesn't want to have a baby, or if pregnancy is a **risk** to her health, she can have an **abortion** if she decides that's the best option for her.

An abortion is the medical process of **ending a pregnancy** so it doesn't result in the birth of a baby, either by taking medication or having a small surgical procedure.

Whether or not a woman wants to do this is a very **personal** decision and can be affected by all sorts of things, like her cultural background, the circumstances of the pregnancy, and her feelings about having children.

CONTRACEPTION

If and when you feel emotionally, mentally, and physically ready to have sex, it is important to stay safe. You and your partner need to protect yourselves from sexually transmitted infections (known as STIs) and from unwanted or unexpected pregnancy. There are lots of ways to do this, and you and your partner can choose a way that suits you both.

Condoms offer the most effective protection against STIs. They are 98 percent effective at preventing **pregnancy**. By using **condoms** alongside a **second** form of contraception, you can be confident that STIs and unexpected pregnancy are very unlikely.

Even though most forms of contraception are designed for women and girls to use, contraception choices are the **responsibility** of BOTH partners. It's important for boys to be aware of the pros and cons of the different options so they can support their partners.

Do I have an STI?

Many STIs don't cause **symptoms**. Once you are **sexually active**, the only way to be sure that you are not carrying an STI is to visit a **doctor** or sexual health **clinic** where they can do some quick, easy tests. Don't feel embarrassed. The staff there want to make sure you are **safe and well**, and won't judge you. And if you do have an STI, there are safe and effective **treatments** available.

Always discuss with your partner which methods of contraception you are planning to use. If you are unsure how any of the methods work or which one to use, or you just need some reassurance or have any questions, discuss your options with a medical professional (your doctor, a school nurse) or visit a family planning clinic or sexual health clinic.

The safest way to have sex is to use BOTH condoms AND another method of contraception at the same time.

Condom:

thin, latex cover that fits snugly over man's erect penis. When the man ejaculates inside the woman's vagina, the condom catches and collects the sperm to stop them entering the fallopian tubes.

Pros: Easy to get (shop or clinic) and the best way to protect against STIs.

Cons: If not used correctly can come off or split during sex. Can only be used once.

Contraceptive implant:

A small, plastic rod placed under the skin in a woman's upper arm. It releases hormones to prevent pregnancy.

Pros: 99 percent effective, lasts for 3 years.

Cons: Must be inserted by a doctor. Can affect a girl's period cycle. Doesn't protect against STIs.

Diaphragm

flexible rubber dome that is inserted into woman's vagina to cover the cervix.

Pros: Reusable after it is washed.

Cons: Difficult to use. Not as effective as condoms. Requires a doctor visit to ensure the device fits properly and is being used correctly. Does not protect against STIs.

The pill:

A tablet that girls take containing hormones to prevent pregnancy. There are several different types.

Pros: 99 percent effective, and may also reduce period pain and symptoms.

Cons: Must be taken every day. Not effective if she forgets to take it, or if she is sick or has diarrhea. Doesn't protect against STIs.

Contraceptive injection:

An injection of hormones which prevent pregnancy.

Pros: 99 percent effective, lasts up to 12 weeks.

Cons: Must be given by a doctor. Doesn't protect against STIs.

IUD (Intrauterine device, or coil)

A small, T-shaped device that's put into the cervix. It releases either copper or hormones to stop pregnancy.

Pros: 99 percent effective, works for between 5 and 10 years.

Cons: Doesn't protect against STIs. Can affect a girl's periods.

Emergency contraception

If you have **unprotected sex,** or if your contraceptive method **fails** (for example, condom splits or you miss taking your pill), **emergency contraception** can still prevent pregnancy. This is usually in the form of a **pill** or an **IUD,** available from a doctor or sexual health clinic. It needs to be given as soon as possible after sex.

DO i HAVE TO DO iT?

The law around consent

The law on consent is there to **protect you** and make sure you are not made to do anything you **don't want** to do. Different states have different 'ages of consent': the age at which you are legally able to agree to have sex.

If someone **over the age of consent** has sex or does sexual things with you when you are younger than the age of consent, **with or without your agreement**, they can be **arrested** for assault and rape.

Whatever your age, if someone has sex or does sexual things with you **without your consent**, they can be arrested for assault and rape.

T he answer is always 'no!' You are entitled to set your own boundaries within your relationships. This means you are always able to say 'no' when something makes you uncomfortable.

You decide for yourself about what you're **comfortable** with in a relationship. These decisions make up a set of boundaries personal to you.

Your boundaries may be different with different people. For example, you might be fine with a friend giving you a hug, while preferring to keep your distance from someone you've just met. And not all boundaries are **physical** or **sexual**. Some are **emotional**, or relate to **privacy**. For example, you might prefer it if your friend doesn't use your phone without your permission. Or you might be fine with it. It's **up to you**.

Discuss boundaries with your partners, friends, and family. Their boundaries may be different from yours. You have a **right** to have your boundaries respected, and a **responsibility** to respect the boundaries of people around you. **Never** pressure anyone to do anything that crosses their boundaries.

Sexual boundaries and consent

Sexual consent means giving permission, **without pressure or fear**, to be involved in anything sexual. This includes having sex, touching, or taking pictures. Sex without your agreement is always illegal, however old you are. You can't **legally** consent to have sex or do sexual things with another person while you are under the age of consent.

Sexual feelings can be quite strong, but **no one has the right** to make you do anything sexual that you are not comfortable with. That includes sexual acts to your body or theirs, whether you are in the same place or using technology to connect. It's **up to you** what sexual activities you consent to. That includes the decision **not to have sex**.

You also have a **responsibility** to respect your partner's sexual boundaries. **Always** ask for consent before any sexual activity and be sure it's been given **freely,** without fear or worry about upsetting you, and hasn't been influenced by alcohol or drugs. If someone refuses or withdraws consent, **stop** what you're doing, **respect** their decision, and **don't pressure** them to change their mind.

Can I change my mind?

Yes. Always. Consent **isn't** a **forever** thing. You can **change your mind** if you start to feel uncomfortable at any time. If you consent to something, you don't have to agree to take things any further or do anything else.

What is sexting?

Sexting is the sending and receiving of naked **pictures** of your body or parts of your body ('nudes'), pictures of you in underwear, sexual pictures, **videos** or live streams of your body, or sexually explicit **messages**. To have or send sexual pictures or videos, including selfies, **legally** you have to be over the age of 18. If you are being pressured or **bullied** into sending pictures, talk to someone as soon as you can.

If you have sent pictures and **something goes wrong** (for example, if you accidentally send them to the wrong person, or if they get **shared** without your permission), talk to a trusted adult and ask the other person to **delete** the pictures. You might feel guilty, embarrassed, or frightened, but whatever has happened, you deserve **respect** and **support**. If someone has betrayed your trust, **it is not your fault for trusting them**.

If you've sent them to someone at **school**, ask a parent or member of staff to help you. The school can investigate and take the phone away from the person if necessary. If a naked picture of you ends up on a **website** and you're under 18, you can report it to the website to have it removed.

Whatever your age, never send sexts to someone without their consent. This can count as harassment if the other person feels upset or violated by the messages.

KEEPING CLEAN

Your body is like any machine: it needs to be taken care of if it's going to work properly. As you go through puberty, you'll have to get used to carrying out a few extra pieces of routine maintenance to keep yourself clean and healthy.

Sweat

A side effect of the changes in your body is that you'll start to **sweat** more, and your sweat will have a stronger smell than it used to.

Everyone has sweat glands all over their body. There are **clusters** of them under your armpits and around your genitals, so extra sweat builds up in these areas. Although sweat doesn't have much of a **smell** when it's fresh, it does start to develop an odor if it sits around for a while.

For this reason, you need to **wash** your body, and in particular your armpits and genitals, more frequently during and after puberty. You will need to make sure you change your **clothes** a lot more than you did before, especially your underwear and socks. A bit of **deodorant** is very handy for reducing how much you sweat, and getting rid of sweaty smells. You can get spray-on, roll-on, or deodorant sticks. Try a few and see what works for you.

Look after the basics

Growing up is **exhausting**. The changes taking place in your growing body use up a lot of energy, so it is really important to make sure you get enough **sleep**. You can find more information about good sleeping patterns on page 62.

Eating well is also essential to keeping you healthy. Your body needs the right variety of foods in the right balance. Make sure your diet includes a good range of vitamins, minerals, sugars, fats, protein, and carbohydrate.

You also need to make sure you have time to **relax**. You may feel that life has suddenly got very busy, with schoolwork, friends, family, and hobbies all demanding your attention. Make sure you allow some time to be **calm** and **quiet** now and then. See page 68 for more information.

Keeping active

Everybody tends to put on **weight** during puberty. This is a natural part of your body's growth. Keeping active and doing regular **exercise** will help you keep a steady body weight, one that is right for you. Exercise will also help to build up your **muscles** and **bones** and keep them strong.

Exercise doesn't need to be **boring** or a chore. Join a sports **club** or team at school, or go running or on **walks** with your friends. As well as being good for you, **exercise** is also a great way to meet new people. And you will feel better, not just physically, but also **mentally**.

sleep

eat right

relax

You or some of your friends may have experimented with tobacco, alcohol, or even drugs. It is important to understand the dangers of doing this, and the risks you are taking. See page 54 for more information.

What about Drugs?

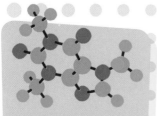

The law

There are laws to **protect** you and your health while you're still growing. Different states have different laws and age restrictions when it comes to buying and consuming alcohol, tobacco products, and drugs. Be aware of the laws in your state. If you're worried about anything, ask for help.

During adolescence, some people are drawn to trying things that seem exciting, such as smoking, drinking, vaping, taking drugs, or hanging out with people who are doing those things. Not everyone feels this pressure, but if you do, it's important to know the facts and the risks.

Because of the changes your brain is going through, you might find yourself acting more **impulsively**, taking more **risks,** and sometimes having poor judgment and insight for a while. Because of this, you may be more likely to want to try **alcohol** and **drugs**. But these changes also mean that your brain will react more strongly to them, and this could make you more **vulnerable**.

Wanting to **impress** your peers can sometimes mean you do things you wouldn't usually do, or that you regret later. Decide what your own **values** and boundaries are, and don't get pressured into doing anything you don't want to do. You're **responsible** for your own actions and if something goes wrong, it's you who has to deal with the consequences, even if your peers encouraged you.

Sometimes people use **substances** to cover up difficult **feelings** instead of finding healthy ways to cope with them. If you think that may be the case for you, talk to someone who can help or call one of the help lines at the back of this book.

How do they work?

Whenever you're doing something you enjoy, your brain makes a chemical called **dopamine** (a neurotransmitter). You have receptors all over your brain that grab these chemicals as they float past, increasing your sense of **pleasure**. In adolescence, these receptors are extra **sensitive**. Drugs can fit into these receptors, which is why they can make you feel good until they wear off. This good feeling is **temporary**, and usually followed by a period of time when you feel much **worse** (a 'comedown.')

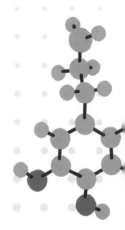

Alcohol fits into other receptors in your brain. It lowers your **inhibitions**, which may make you feel more confident (but may also mean you do things you regret once you're sober). It also affects the part of your brain that handles **balance** and coordination, which is why it makes you clumsy. Large amounts of alcohol can make you sick and cause serious **illness**.

What are the risks?

There are different risks associated with ifferent drugs. Some drugs can be harmful even **deadly**. Some can kill you on the st use, while others can cause **long-term** ealth conditions. You can find lots of reliable formation about specific drugs and where to d support by going to the **NIDA** website (see e link at the back of this book).

Even caffeine in coffee and energy drinks has an effect on your brain chemistry. As a teen, you are more sensitive to these effects, some of which may make you feel quite uncomfortable or affect your behavior.

It's also important to remember that, with illegal bstances, the people who make and sell them nnot be **trusted**. This means it's impossible to be sure actly **what** and **how much** you are taking. This may mean you n take more of a substance than you were intending or expecting to. The drugs ay also have been mixed with other **dangerous** substances.

When you are less **in control** of your thoughts and behavior because of ugs or alcohol, you may find yourself in **unsafe** situations without the vareness to protect yourself.

Mental health conditions like depression or anxiety may get worse s a result of substance abuse, and users may be more likely to evelop mental illness. Cannabis (weed) can cause paranoia, for xample, while other drugs can cause perception disorders.

People can feel unable to cope without the drug or alcohol and their life volves around getting more of it. The drug then controls them, and is is called **addiction**. Addiction is hard to break.

If you or someone you know has taken something and you're worried about their safety, get medical advice immediately. Be honest and upfront with paramedics and doctors about what you or they have taken. They won't tell the police or get you in trouble, but it may help them save your or your friend's life.

UNDER PRESSURE

E ducation can be stressful. Lots of people worry about learning, remembering, organizing homework, and taking exams. You may find it difficult to manage your schoolwork while fitting in your social life, hobbies, and time to relax, as well as managing relationships with peers and adults.

During adolescence, you will be more **in charge** of managing your life and your schoolwork than you were when you were younger. This is a good thing; it's all part of growing up and becoming **independent**. But it can be hard work.

Your brain is already very busy with all the changes it is making. It might struggle sometimes with planning, organizing and doing **schoolwork**. This will change in time. There have been many disorganized teens who've grown into superorganized adults. You're still learning and developing, and **organization** is a skill in its own right. Find what works for you: writing lists, having a notebook, or filling out a planning chart or timetable are just some things you could try.

Schoolwork and homework can cause **stress**, especially if you don't understand what you need to do or if you have too much of it to cope with. It's important to ask for help when you need it. Talk to friends to check task instructions, and, if you need to, talk to your **teachers** and explain the problem. Good teachers will be supportive of you: they want you to succeed and fulfill your **potential**, whatever that potential looks like.

Learning difficulties

If you have a **learning difficulty** like dyslexia, dyspraxia, dysgraphia, dyscalculia, epilepsy, cerebral palsy, ADHD, or autism, you will have extra challenges. Try not to get frustrated. Ask for help, extra time, and the right **support**, such as using technology. Take your time and try the triangle breathing exercise (page 57) to keep you calm and **focused**.

Exam stress

If you're feeling stressed about **exams,** you are not alone! Exams make people stressed all over the world. Here are some tips to keep you relaxed and positive.

Breathe slowly and remind yourself that you're doing your best. You are stronger and smarter than your anxiety or stress.

No one's whole future depends on an exam result. Exams are important, but they're not a one-time thing. You can often resit exams if you need to.

Study little and often: no more than 45 minutes in one block. Take regular breaks, eat healthy snacks, and drink water. Go outside for 15 minutes if you can between revision blocks.

Picture yourself walking into the exam calmly, turning over the paper with a smile, and writing down what you know. Believe in yourself. You've got this!

Remember, there are hundreds of skills and talents that exams don't measure, and there is no one way to be happy and successful.

Moving schools can be particularly stressful, but the thought of it is generally worse than the change itself. You might worry about finding your way around, the work being too hard, or the teachers being different. You've probably worried about these things before and then found it was **fine**. The work will get harder, but you'll be getting older and **smarter**. And there will always be people around to **support** you when you need it.

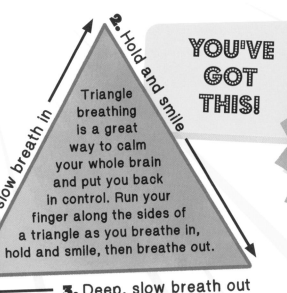

2. Hold and smile

Slow breath in

Triangle breathing is a great way to calm your whole brain and put you back in control. Run your finger along the sides of a triangle as you breathe in, hold and smile, then breathe out.

3. Deep, slow breath out

YOU'VE GOT THIS!

An anxious mind will find studying more difficult. If you're finding that worries keep distracting you in class, let your teachers know so they can adapt the information and lessons for you. Don't worry about next week or next year or the future; stick with what's happening now, and breathe!

BODY IMAGE

B ody image is how we think and feel about ourselves physically, and how we believe others see us. Your body image may change, depending on all sorts of things, from your mood to the images you see and how people treat you.

It is important to remember that there are **many forms** of beauty and attractiveness and everyone has a **different** view of what is appealing. What you find attractive in others might be different from what other people find **attractive** in you.

It is also important to remember that how you look is only a **very small part** of who you are. You are valued and loved for so many reasons that go far beyond your physical appearance.

Why's everyone looking at me?

It's normal in adolescence to feel more aware of your body and how you look. You may find that you're **comparing** your body to other people's more often, to see how it is the same or different. These feelings affect everyone in adolescence, and can sometimes make you feel out of control or **anxious**.

You might feel like everyone is looking at you and that they are evaluating and **judging** you. When you feel self-conscious about your body, you may get embarrassed easily and feel uncomfortable in your own skin.

The changes in your body can also play a part. As you grow taller and your body shape changes, your brain may get **confused** as, for a while, it may not know exactly where your limbs are. You may use too much force in your movements, or not enough, because your brain can't calculate what's needed as well as it used to. This can make you feel **awkward** and clumsy. Don't worry, it won't be long before your brain has mapped everything out and is back in charge.

How can I feel better about how I look?

★ Don't be fooled by magazine images or selfies that have been **filtered** and **edited** to make people look 'perfect.' They are not real.

★ Work out what you **like** about yourself and which parts of you you're **happy** with. Write them down and stick them onto your **mirror**, so you're reminded of them whenever you look at yourself.

Be around friends and family who make you feel **positive** about yourself. Remember, you are valued for many reasons.

If you are worried about part of your body or you're feeling **overwhelmed**, talk to someone you trust, one of the counselors on a support website, or your doctor. They're there to help.

You rock!

What if I hate the way I look?

If you feel like you hate the way you look, you may be experiencing **body dysmorphia**. Because of the way the brain develops in adolescence, sometimes people see themselves very differently from how others see them. It's like an **optical illusion** where their eyes trick them into seeing themselves differently than how they really are. They find it really hard to believe others when they say nice things about them. This can affect their feelings of control and self-esteem. Body dysmorphia is **treatable,** so if it happens to you, talk to someone and get help.

Sometimes, because they are unhappy with the way they look or because something else in their life is making them unhappy, people lose control of how much or how little they eat.

This can have very serious health consequences. **Eating disorders** are common and can affect anyone of any body shape or lifestyle.

Being anxious or **stressed** can trigger eating problems. While your brain and body are changing, you might feel like you have no control over your own life and body, so controlling what or how much you eat can give you back that feeling of order.

It can be hard to accept that you might have an eating problem. Accepting that the problem exists will help you start to recover. If you are experiencing difficulties with your body image, it's important to know you are not alone. Look up some **support groups** on the websites listed in the resources section.

Your eyes are easily fooled. Are these lines and dots the same or are they different? When you've decided, measure them to find out.

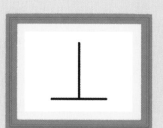

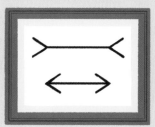

STRESS

Feelings of anxiety or stress can be more intense during puberty. It is important to find healthy ways to manage these feelings so they don't get in your way for long.

Feeling **stressed** can be physically uncomfortable and emotionally upsetting. You might notice tightness in your **body** or a real mix of feelings in your **mind**. You could feel more worried, anxious, scared or overwhelmed than usual without any obvious reason. Things that are a bit annoying can make you upset, angry, and unreasonable, which you regret a short while later.

The good news is that you can quickly learn to **control** this when you understand it. There are some really effective ways to elbow worry out of your way and feel chilled and calm. Master these now and you'll find it easier to cope later.

What's my brain doing?

Sometimes people might say you have nothing to stress about. Gently remind them to read this book so they can remember what your **brain** is undertaking and how many **changes** it's making. Your changing, growing brain sometimes gets a blip, and like anything that's working hard, sometimes it blows a fuse! You can't turn it off then on again like a glitchy computer, but a little **understanding** and relaxation can go a long way to fixing things.

All the stress **hormones** your overworked brain is creating to help you mature can make it feel like there are lots of things to worry about. School, friends, family, and self-confidence can all be a cause of stress, along with many other things.

On top of this, an ancient part of your brain called the **limbic system** (see page 10) experiences changes during puberty, which can make you more **sensitive** to stress and less good at taking the best care of yourself. Too much stress can affect your thinking skills and ability to make **good decisions** and healthy choices. It's important to take time to **manage** your stress and not ignore your mind if it hurts.

> Bad feelings will pass. They're just traffic in your mind and body. Don't let them park in your brain!

YOU CAN BEAT STRESS

What do I need to do?

To combat stress, your brain needs some quality downtime. Here are some fabulous, fast stress fixers:

★ Find a calm, quiet spot where you can relax. Breathe in and out deeply for three minutes. In time with your in-breath, say in your head 'breathe in calm' and in time with your out-breath, say 'breathe out stress.' Now, imagine a place where you could feel totally safe and comfortable, maybe somewhere you've seen, been to, heard about, read about, or dreamed about. It's a special safe place where everything feels peaceful, calm, and secure. Spend 10 to 15 minutes observing all the things you love in this safe place. Draw it if you feel like it.

★ Make up a silly song or sing your favorite song in a silly voice. It will remind your brain to have a giggle as well as work hard.

★ **SSS**: cut out **S**ugar, focus on your **S**trengths, and get some **S**leep!

★ **Exercise** and **enjoy nature:** sometimes we need to remember that we are part of a bigger world which is incredible and awesome, just like you are!

★ **Talk 12**: Talk to someone for 12 minutes about anything you like. It doesn't have to be about your worries, but it can be if you like. Otherwise, hobbies, sports, fashion, animals, comics, books, music, and films all make for good conversations.

★ Make a point of looking after yourself physically when you're stressed out. A bit of **rest** and a **healthy meal** can go a long way.

There are more stress-busting activities on page 68. Everyone is different, and what works for one person may not work so well for someone else, so try a few different things to find out which techniques suit you best.

Do i have to sleep?

Teenagers need more sleep than children or adults because of the extra power the brain uses while it's developing. You'll probably need to sleep for about 9¼ hours a night.

Although you need more sleep as a teenager, you may find it's more difficult to **fall asleep**. During adolescence, your brain's sense of day and night **changes** by a few hours. This makes it harder to fall asleep before around 11pm. It also makes it hard to wake up and get going in the morning.

On **weekends**, it's not unusual for teenagers to sleep in for most of the morning as they catch up on the rest they've missed during the week. If your body needs 9 or 10 hours of sleep a night, and you're only getting 7 or 8, then over a school week, you can end up **losing** up to 15 hours of sleep.

Not getting enough sleep is called **sleep deprivation**, something that has been used as a form of torture because it's so unpleasant. It makes you **emotional** and irritable, and less able to learn or focus your attention. Too little sleep can affect your **mood** and your memory, make anxiety worse, and slow down your brain's **development**. So it's important to **prioritize** rest as much as you can.

How can I get to sleep?

Here are some things that can help you to fall asleep and stay asleep:

★ Avoid backlit screens in the hour before bed. The light delays the hormones your brain needs to release so you can fall asleep.

★ Spend time in natural light during the day and in low-level light before bed. This helps your brain with its day and night cycles.

★ Avoid heavy meals before bed. It can help to have a small snack of carbohydrate and protein; a bowl of non-sugary cereal and milk (or vegan milk) is ideal.

★ Put on some warm socks. If your feet are toasty, it makes you fall asleep more quickly. Try it!

★ Develop a routine to wind down. Maybe take a bath or shower, then put on some relaxing music and read for a while.

★ Do a relaxation exercise like the ones at the back of this book. Keep doing it for 20 minutes or until you're fast asleep.

What happens when I sleep?

Your **brain** is just as busy while you're asleep as when you're awake. It is consolidating your day's learning, putting things into your **memory** stores, pruning old pathways you no longer need, and **cleaning** out any waste that's been generated.

A good way to **make the most** of your brain's night-time activity is to go over some learning just before you fall asleep. It will get wired into your brain more quickly and for longer.

Sleep is also important for your **physical health**. It helps the cells in your body and muscles to recover and heal from injury and illness.

Keep a sleep diary for a week. Work out how many hours you get out of the total 63-70 hours you need.

Sleep diary

Day 1:

Day 2:

Day 3:

Day 4:

Day 5:

Day 6:

Day 7:

WHAT'S UP?

Growing up is hard. There may be times when you feel confused, upset, or worried by some of the changes you experience. Everyone does from time to time. It's normal to feel down, to question yourself, and to lose confidence for a while.

This book explains lots of the things you may have to deal with and will help you to **understand** your feelings, make **choices** about how to react, talk to others about your worries (if you want to), and be **happy** to be you.

If your low mood **sticks around**, or your worries get so big that you start to avoid doing things you need to do or used to enjoy, you may need more **help**. Don't worry: you are not alone. We all know that bodies can become unwell. Your **mind** can become unwell, too. Just like with physical illnesses, you need to get **treatment** and support.

Remember, there is help and treatment available. Recognizing mental health issues early can help to stop them from getting worse, but it's never too late to ask for support.

What is mental health?

When your mind is working as it should, you have good mental health. If things start to feel out of balance, if you feel upset all the time or you struggle to know what is real and what isn't, your mental health may need some treatment. One in four people across the world have a mental health problem at any one time. There are treatments available, and having a problem now doesn't mean you'll always have it.

Understanding some of the most common mental health issues will allow you to recognize them if you or a friend start to experience them. Common mental health problems include:

★ **Anxiety or panic:** when you get so worried about things that it gets in the way of your life. Panic feels like you can't cope and are overwhelmed by fear.

If you feel you're in need of help or if you're worried about anything on this page, talk to someone you trust. Your parents, school nurse, school staff, doctors, youth workers, and other

PTSD: when you have a deeply frightening experience and it doesn't fade with time.

Depression: when you feel down for more than a couple of weeks and nothing makes you feel better. You can find it difficult to be bothered to do anything.

Eating disorders: when eating too much or too little becomes a problem for your health.

Mood disorders: when your mood changes frequently, and you go from feeling too high to too low in cycles, or you feel too high or too long.

OCD: when you have distressing thoughts, images, or feelings and need everything to be done a certain way so you feel better or 'just right' again.

Perception disorders: when reality is different for you than how others perceive it. You might feel muddled, or not know if you are dreaming, or if something is really happening. You might hear, smell, see, or feel things that aren't there.

Are you worried? List what you're worried about, and how long it's been going on for. Then share it with someone. You don't have to tell them everything if you're not ready.

YOU ARE NOT ALONE

trusted adults can arrange for you to speak to someone for advice, or you can use some of the resources and help lines on page 70. Nothing will be new to them, even if it feels that way to you. They have talked to thousands of children and teens with every imaginable problem. They will know how to help you, and there are websites with a great range of support.

BeiNG Me

How can I feel more confident?

Y ou're awesome. You're also not perfect: perfect isn't possible. Striving to be perfect is unhealthy and will always end in disappointment. Focus more on finding the ways you are awesome and unique. You might surprise yourself.

You **will** make **mistakes**. Lots of them. **Celebrate** them as a chance to **learn** more about yourself. Mistakes have led to some of the **best** inventions, like fire, medicines, plastic, and microwave ovens. Maybe you know something you can do now because you made mistakes; can you think of anything?

Keep this book handy and reread the information you need any time you like. And when you're done with this phase of your life, pass on the book and your knowledge!

Curiouser and curiouser...

Be **curious** about the world and about yourself. This means looking for **understanding, ideas,** and **questions** about your life, feelings, thoughts, and actions. It's **ok** not to have **all the answers** and to not know what you believe or think about things. You may not have all the information you need, yet. It's better to **take your time** and investigate than to jump to definite answers too quickly. You have all of your life to work things out.

Recognizing this will make you feel more **resilient** when things go wrong or when you make mistakes. If you discover you've been wrong, think about what led you to the wrong decision. You'll learn more about yourself by working out **why** you think something than if you simply work out **what** you think.

Pay attention to what you think about yourself and **challenge negative thoughts** as they pop up. It's healthy to recognize what you can do better and where you have room for improvement. But not all negative thoughts are helpful, and some of them are just plain wrong. You don't have to believe every thought you have about yourself.

If a negative thought or unhelpful belief comes up, try asking these questions:

1. Is it true?
2. What's the evidence?
3. What else could it mean?

Imagine your friend had this belief about themselves and tell yourself what you'd tell them. It's often a lot easier to be kind to a friend than it is to be kind to yourself.

MISTAKES ARE THE MAKERS OF SUCCESS

Making changes

Confidence tends to take a knock during puberty, but you can build it back up by setting yourself small, achievable **goals** and making little changes to your life and routine. Little changes and small goals build up to make a big difference.

Choose a **goal** that you'd like to achieve, like keeping your room clean for a week, phoning your grandparents every Tuesday, or starting a new club.

★ write your goal down

★ decide what steps you need to take to make it happen

★ decide how you will know if you succeeded

★ decide how to reward yourself for achieving it

★ do it!

★ Repeat...

GOAL:

TO DO:

RESULT SHOULD BE:

REWARD:

START DATE:

HOW CAN i RELAX?

Relaxation is vital to keeping your body, brain, and mind healthy. Relaxing can take practice. If you've been very anxious or stressed, it may feel a bit strange, but keep trying and you'll start to feel better; more focused, more confident, and more in control. You don't have to do all of these activities. Choose the ones that work well for you.

3:5 breathing

This works wherever you are and whatever you are doing. The best part is no one even knows you're doing it, so if you need to cool down without being noticed, give it a go. If you're by yourself you could close your eyes while you do it.

Get comfortable in a sitting position. Notice your body breathing in and out. After a few breaths, start to count along with yourself, making your in-breath last for the count of 3 and your out-breath last for the count of 5, breathing smoothly. Got it? Great! Keep going for as long you want, or until you feel calm again.

Practicing this every day will help make it more effective when you really need it.

Cool hands

Pick a quiet, calm spot and lay down. Close your eyes and picture yourself in a lovely, warm place. Breathe deeply and slowly. Now, focus all your attention on your hands and imagine you are holding a bag of ice cubes. Notice your hands start to actually feel cooler. When you've mastered this skill, try spreading the chilly feeling up your arms and down into your tummy. You'll be calm in no time!

Star fingers

This is a really 'handy' skill!

Spread your hand out like a star on your knee or on a table. Notice your body breathing in and out. Take your pointer finger from the opposite hand, put it on the bottom of your thumb, and begin to slowly trace up along the outside, breathing in as you go. Stop at your thumbnail and hold your breath for a second, then trace back down the other side of your thumb while breathing out.

Now do this again with the next finger. Keep going until you've traced every finger. See how smoothly you can trace your whole hand, keeping your breathing smooth.

Repeat this six times, remembering to keep all your attention on your hand and your breath.

Heart healer

Slowing down your heart rate is really good for your brain and body.

Go outside and find something natural that's living, moving, or growing. It could be a flower or an insect, or even the clouds or the moon. Start off by checking your pulse and notice how fast it's going. Now focus on watching your natural thing for 1 or 2 minutes (or longer if you like). Don't do anything except notice the thing you are looking at. Look at it as if you are seeing it for the very first time ever. Then find three more things and repeat the activity. Check your pulse again right at the end and see if it's slowed down. Notice how you are feeling now.

Taking your pulse:

Take your first two fingers of either hand, place them gently on your wrist or on your throat, just off to one side. If you can't feel the rhythm of your pulse, try the other side; it's definitely there somewhere! You can feel how many times it 'pumps' in a minute. This is your heart rate.

HOW CaN i Get heLP?

Everyone needs some extra support sometimes. There are lots of ways to access this support, and you never have to feel alone.

Often, the best place to start is to talk to a parent. Most parents want to support their children as much as they can. If there's something bothering you, taking the time to sit and talk through it with them might help you to start feeling better. They might have some good advice, too.

Trusted adults

If you'd rather not talk to your parents about something, you may want to speak to other trusted adults in your life. This might be:

an older relative,

a teacher,

a school counselor,

your school nurse,

your doctor or nurse,

a sexual health clinician,

your therapist

a youth worker, social worker or religious adviser.

You know best who you feel comfortable talking to. Don't feel like you're bothering them or that they're not interested in helping you. You matter more to them than you might think!

Other resources

Sometimes, you may not feel like you want to talk face-to-face, or that you'd rather speak to a stranger than someone who knows you. Other times, you may feel you need support straight away, and you can't wait to see someone. Or you may just want a bit more information on how to deal with something in this book. In all these cases, there are lots of resources available. You don't have to deal with things on your own.

American SPCC advice on bullying

(https://americanspcc.org/our-voice/bullying/)

A good source of information on bullying, explaining the different forms, and offering advice on how to deal with it for victims, perpetrators, and witnesses.

hildhelp
(ww.childhelp.org)
hone: 1-800 422-4453

hildhelp is dedicated to looking
fter children who are being
bused or at risk of abuse.
heir free, confidential help line
uts you in touch with a counselor
ny time, day or night.

yber Tipline
(ww.missingkids.org/gethelpnow/
bertipline)

his site offers step-by-step
dvice on how to get personal
ages removed from social
edia and other websites. It
so has a service to report any
cidents where an adult is trying
groom someone who is
derage (that is, manipulate
em into a sexual situation,
real life or online).

ational Suicide
revention Lifeline
ttps://suicideprevention
eline.org)
hone: 1-800-273-8255

ree, 24-hour support for anyone
ho feels they are at risk of
icide or self-harm. You can call
ee of charge at any time and be
ut through to a counselor in your
ea who can offer advice and
ipport. There are also articles
the site offering guidance to
ifferers, survivors, and anyone
oncerned about a friend or
ved one.

NEDA (National Eating Disorders Association)
(www.nationaleatingdisorders.org)

NEDA is a network of organizations
dedicated to helping people with eating
disorders. You can find lots of information
on their website, as well as links to sources
of support local to you.

NIDA for Teens
(https://teens.drugabuse.gov/)

The National Institute on Drug Abuse offers
a teen-focused website with clear, detailed
information about substance abuse, including
drugs, tobacco, and alcohol. You can read
about the different types of substances,
how they affect users' health and wellbeing,
and how to get help if you or anyone
you know needs it.

TeensHealth
(https://kidshealth.org/en/teens)

Offers a wide range of articles with advice
on puberty and sexual health,
as well as answers to general questions
about your body and health issues.

iNDeX